John the Baptist
Forerunner of Jesus

JOANNIE HUMAN • ILLUSTRATED BY JAMES PADGETT

BROADMAN PRESS
Nashville, Tennessee

Dewey Decimal Classification: J232.94
Subject heading: JOHN THE BAPTIST
Printed in the United States of America

Contents

A Son Promised

"What is it, Zacharias? What is wrong?" The smile of welcome on Elizabeth's face turned to a look of concern, then fear. Her husband, a priest, had just returned from the Temple.

Elizabeth had been alone for a week while Zacharias took his turn as priest in the Temple at Jerusalem. Twice a year he left their home in the hills of Judea to do this special work.

Though Elizabeth and Zacharias had been married for years, they had no children. They had prayed for a child for a long time. Now the hope of becoming parents had grown dim.

Again Elizabeth questioned her husband, "Are you ill? What's the matter?" Elizabeth realized then that her husband had not said a word since he returned.

Zacharias smiled. He looked happier than Elizabeth ever remembered. Zacharias drew his wife to him, holding her close. Still he said nothing.

"Can you not speak? Tell me! What is it?" Elizabeth kept asking.

With signs Zacharias told Elizabeth he could not speak. But he could wait no longer to tell her the exciting news.

Making signs with his hands and writing on a clay tablet, Zacharias began.

"We are going to have a son!" he wrote first.

"How can this be?" Elizabeth asked. "We are too old to become parents."

"Let me tell you. In the Temple I was chosen to do something I had never done before. It fell my lot to burn the incense on the altar. All the people waited outside for me. As I stood praying to God, I realized I was not alone! Gabriel, the angel, stood beside the altar. He told me we would have a son and must name him John.

"And our boy will be a special baby. He is the one God wants to get the people ready for the coming of the Messiah.

"I will not be able to speak until our son is born."

For many months Elizabeth stayed mostly to herself. Seldom did her neighbors see her. She wanted to think about God's promise.

About three months before the baby was born, Mary, Elizabeth's cousin, came to visit. As soon as Mary arrived, Elizabeth somehow knew that Mary was going to tell her something special. Mary was to become the mother of the Messiah.

No one could have been happier than these two women. For weeks they visited together. They praised God. They must have talked about what their sons would do and be.

After Mary went back home, the happy day came for Elizabeth. The new baby—a boy—arrived.

Neighbors came to welcome the new baby. How happy they were that at last Elizabeth and Zacharias had a child.

"You will name him after his father, of course," they said.

"His name is John," Elizabeth declared. "That name means 'The Lord is gracious.' We feel the Lord has been good to us."

Their friends could not believe the baby would be called John. None of the relatives had that name. The friends turned to Zacharias.

They asked him the baby's name. Zacharias called for a writing tablet. He wrote, "His name is John."

Then Zacharias discovered that once again he could speak. He began to praise

8

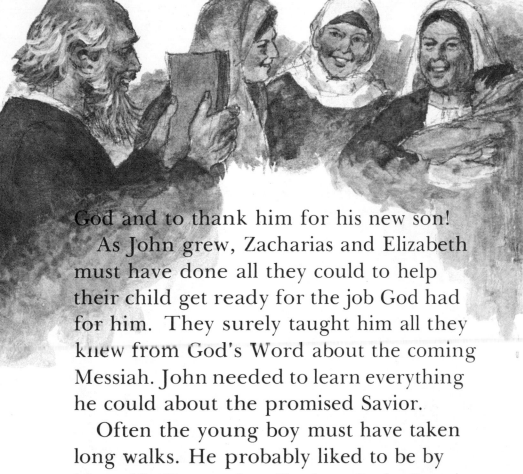

God and to thank him for his new son!

As John grew, Zacharias and Elizabeth must have done all they could to help their child get ready for the job God had for him. They surely taught him all they knew from God's Word about the coming Messiah. John needed to learn everything he could about the promised Savior.

Often the young boy must have taken long walks. He probably liked to be by himself. He surely talked to God often. He seemed to know he had something special to do.

Thinkback: The Bible does not tell us every word Elizabeth and Zacharias said to each other. But we can imagine what they said.

Find in this section and in Luke 1 what the angel said John would do.

A Mission Accepted

The time came for John to leave home so he could prepare himself for his special job. The Bible does not say much about this part of John's life, but it could have happened like this.

"Mother, I think it is time for me to go away," John said. "There is something that I must do, but I am not sure what it is. Perhaps if I go somewhere alone, away from everyone else, and pray and think and listen, God will tell me what to do."

"I know, John, that you must go," Elizabeth replied quietly. "I have known that since before you were born. I'll help you get your things ready before you go."

"I won't need much, Mother. You know I like simple things," John answered.

That night Elizabeth told Zacharias what John had said.

"I knew the time was coming," Zacharias said sadly. "He has been a joy to us. No one could ask for a better son. But he must learn exactly what God wants him

10

to do in preparing the way for the Messiah. Let us help him all we can."

The day for John's departure arrived too soon for his parents. When the family awoke that morning, no one had much to say. Elizabeth gathered a loaf of bread, a hunk of cheese, and a few figs. Lovingly, she packed the food for travel. John did

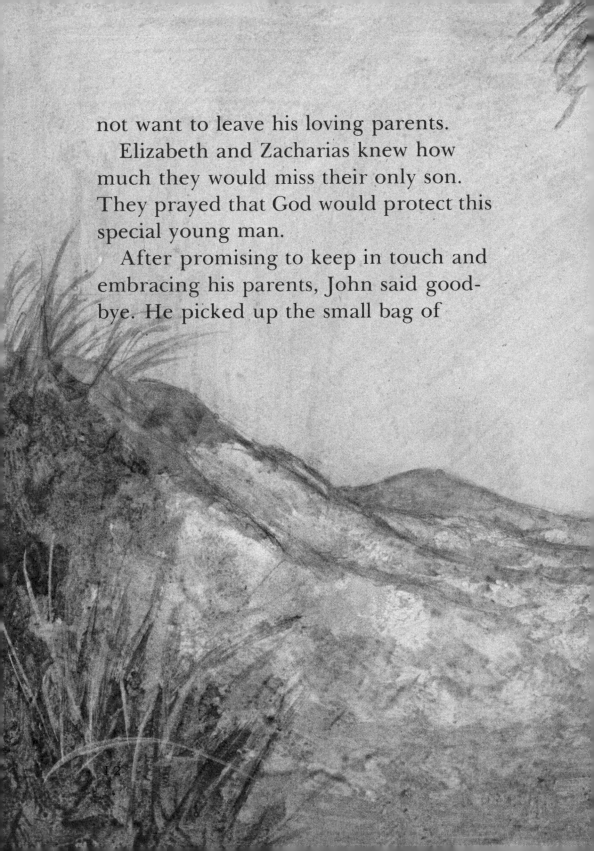

not want to leave his loving parents.

Elizabeth and Zacharias knew how much they would miss their only son. They prayed that God would protect this special young man.

After promising to keep in touch and embracing his parents, John said good-bye. He picked up the small bag of

food and walked swiftly away.

For miles John walked toward the
wilderness near the Jordan River. Once
he stopped to rest and to eat the food his
mother had prepared for him.

John had no idea what he would eat the
next time he became hungry. He did not
know what he would wear when the

13

clothes he had on wore out. The only
thing he knew for sure was that he must
learn what God wanted him to do.

For years John stayed in the wilderness
alone. During this time, God helped him
get ready for a hard job. John knew that
God was telling him that his work was to

get the people ready for the coming of the Messiah.

John thought about the Scriptures he had been taught. He prayed. He listened to God.

When he was hungry, he ate wild honey left by bees in the rocks. He also ate locusts, roasted and salted. For clothing he wore rough, plain robes made from animal skins. He had spent a lot of his boyhood years outdoors and knew how to care for himself.

John did not worry about what he ate or what he wore. He spent his time thinking and preparing himself. He was to be the first prophet God had sent in over four hundred years. He wanted to be sure the message he preached was exactly what God wanted the people to know.

Thinkback: List ways John showed his faith in God. Why did John leave home?

A Ministry Begun

Suddenly, without warning, John the Baptist appeared. He began to preach a message only prophets had spoken before. Crowds of people made their way

to the Jordan River area to hear the new preacher.

"You must repent, for the kingdom of heaven is at hand. The Messiah is coming. You must get ready."

John spoke loudly. He spoke plainly.

There was something about this preacher that made everyone want to listen. His clothes woven of camel's hair were different. But that was not the reason people listened to John. It was his preaching. It was his message that caught the attention of the crowd. He sounded like a prophet.

John the Baptist told the people that they had to change their way of living in order to be ready for the Messiah.

"You must repent and be baptized," John preached boldly.

The people believed John's message. They knew they needed to repent of their sins. They did want to be baptized. And they surely wanted to be ready when the Messiah came. But they wanted John to explain more clearly what he meant.

John told them how to prove they wanted to follow God.

To all the people he said, "Share your food and clothing with those who have none."

To the tax collectors in the crowd, he

warned, "Take from people only the amount of tax that is owed, no more."

To the soldiers there, he said: "Do not punish people wrongly. Do not complain about your pay."

John explained what his kind of baptism meant. His baptism showed that the people who were baptized had changed their minds about their sins and wanted to live clean lives.

"Perhaps this preacher is the Messiah," the people began to say. "We have never heard anyone preach like this. Our people have waited for four hundred years for the Messiah. We had given up hope that he would come."

Someone in the crowd decided to ask John.

"Are you the Messiah?" they called out.

"I am not the Messiah," John the Baptist replied. "When he comes, I will not be worthy even to untie his shoes. I am just a voice crying in the wilderness."

John told the people what he thought the Messiah would do when he came.

John said the Messiah would separate the
good from the bad, just as people
harvesting wheat separated the grain
from the chaff. He said the Messiah's
work was like that of the winnowing fan, a
flat wooden shovel used to toss the grain
into the air to separate it from the chaff.
The chaff would blow away while the
wheat fell to the ground.

John preached that judgment would
come to those who did not repent and

believe in the Messiah.

Many times after John finished preaching people in the crowd walked down into the water to tell John they wanted to repent of their sins and be · baptized. They wanted to show their desire to live good lives.

Day after day, week after week, crowds flocked to the Jordan area to hear John the Baptist. All kinds of people traveled short and long distances to hear this new

22

preacher. Even the religious leaders of Jerusalem joined the throngs of people who went to hear the special messenger of God.

As the multitudes heard John preach, many repented of their sins. People read the Scriptures to learn more about the Messiah. They asked John questions.

John kept preaching. He kept waiting for the Messiah. His message was always the same.

"Repent. The Messiah is coming. You must be ready. You must change your lives!"

Thinkback: Why did crowds of people go to hear John? Why did they think he was the Messiah? What did John tell the people they must do?

The Messiah Named

Every time John preached, he may have wondered if he would meet the Messiah that day. *Will I know him as soon as I see him?* he must have wondered. *Will the Messiah come down from the clouds? Will he come leading an army? Will he even come while I am still alive?*

As the days went by and John continued to preach repentance, many

thoughts and ideas about the Messiah must have filled his mind.

As he preached, perhaps he scanned the crowd, hoping the Messiah stood among the people.

One day John looked up and saw Jesus in the crowd. John had not seen his cousin for years. At that moment, a startling truth crept into John's mind: *Jesus is the Messiah!*

John must have been so excited that he

could hardly keep his mind on what he
was saying. As he finished his sermon,
many came forth to be baptized.

Then he looked up to see Jesus
standing beside him.

"I wish to be baptized, too," Jesus said
quietly to John.

"I cannot baptize you. I'm the one who
should be baptized. Why do you come to
me for baptism?" John asked.

After all, the Messiah did not need to
repent. Jesus did not need forgiveness
from God.

But Jesus insisted. Though he did not need to repent, perhaps he felt that now was the time to let others know who he was. And perhaps he wanted to be an example for people to follow.

For years, Jesus had been preparing for his special work. On that particular day God let John and others know that Jesus was the promised Messiah.

The Messiah asked John to baptize him. John obeyed his Master and baptized him in the waters of the Jordan.

As Jesus was baptized, a voice spoke from heaven, "This is my beloved Son in whom I am well pleased."

John's heart must have filled with joy. The voice from heaven proved it. Jesus

was the Messiah. The Messiah had really come!

Now John and all those around him knew that Jesus was indeed the promised Messiah, the Savior of the world!

John had done a good job preparing the people for the Messiah. People realized they were sinners. They knew they needed to change their minds about sin and repent. They were ready to turn their lives over to Jesus, who had the power to change them into new persons. Only the Messiah could do that.

For several months after Jesus' baptism, John kept preaching. He kept calling people to repent. He kept pointing the way to Jesus. He wanted all people to know the Messiah had come.

John's work was almost finished.

Thinkback: What happened to let John know that Jesus was the Messiah? What did John do with the news? Read John 1:15–34.

The Preacher Arrested

"Repent of your sins!"

John's message was the same for everyone—the poor, the rich, the lowest slave, and the highest ruler of the land. When John saw sin, he condemned it, regardless of who the sinner was.

Even the ruler did not escape John's message. When Herod, the governor of Galilee, broke the law, John condemned him. John declared bluntly that Herod sinned by taking the wife of his brother and marrying her.

Herod would not allow such preaching to continue. After all, who was this preacher to tell the ruler how to act?

31

Herod's soldiers arrested John. They threw him into a dungeon cell at Herod's palace near the shores of the Dead Sea.

Alone and confused, John sat in his cell day after day, thinking. He knew that he had preached what God had told him to preach. He knew that the message he preached was true. Yet, he was in prison, unable to roam the country he loved or preach the message God called him to give.

33

What went wrong? Why am I in prison? What good can I do here? Will the Messiah come and rescue me? Surely the Messiah will raise an army and conquer Herod and free me from prison!

These thoughts kept ringing in his mind. He must have prayed every day to be set free so he could preach. Still nothing happened.

One day John's followers came to the prison to visit their beloved friend. They told him about the things Jesus was doing.

John listened carefully. He knew Jesus was doing good, but *is that what the Messiah*

35

is supposed to do? he must have wondered.
Maybe the Messiah's job was not what
John had expected! Or maybe Jesus was
not the Messiah after all.

"Go to Jesus," he told his followers.
"Ask him if he really is the Messiah. Ask
him if we should keep expecting the
Messiah to come."

The disciples left to find Jesus. Alone in
his cell again, John's thoughts must have
increased his doubts.

John felt cut off from all the action. He
probably thought he was forgotten by

everyone, including Jesus. While Herod
and his wicked wife, Herodias, reigned
over the land, John, a preacher of right
living, was confined to the dungeon.

John's disciples found Jesus while he
was helping people. They asked him,
"Are you the Messiah, or should we look
for another?"

Jesus kept working. The disciples
watched Jesus. They waited for his
answer.

Jesus healed people of their illnesses.
Then he gave his answer for John.

"Go back and tell John what you have seen. The blind see. The lame walk. The lepers return home. The dead live. And even the poor hear my message."

Jesus was letting John know that his work was different from what John had expected.

"I am not raising an army to overcome the government. I am going in and out among the people, meeting needs as I see them. I am showing God's love for his people."

Jesus wanted John to trust him and to understand the work he was doing. Jesus must have felt that John needed to know that being right with God is more important than being right with a government.

John's messengers left. Jesus turned to the crowd once more.

"Who did you go to the wilderness to see?" he asked. "Not a man afraid to speak his message. Not a man stylishly dressed. But you went to hear a prophet who spoke plainly and powerfully, a man who lived by what he preached.

"Do you know who John is?" the Master asked. "He is the one Malachi told us would come to prepare the way for the Messiah. John was sent by God with his message."

John was the forerunner Malachi had said would come. Jesus had proclaimed it!

Then Jesus gave his greatest recorded tribute to a person.

"There is not a greater prophet than John the Baptist," he declared.

As the forerunner of Jesus, John the Baptist became the last prophet to point the way to Jesus. Once Jesus came, there was no need for a prophet. Jesus fulfilled God's promise of a Savior.

Thinkback: List ideas John had about what the Messiah would do. List things the Messiah did. Why do you think John may not have understood Jesus' work?

The Job Completed

At last Herodias, the wicked wife of Herod, had her chance! Since the day Herod had thrown the outspoken John into the dungeon, Herodias had waited for a way to destroy the fiery preacher.

Full of revenge, she waited for the right opportunity to give John the Baptist what she thought he deserved. She would not rest until he was stopped forever from preaching!

    She had vowed that she would get even
with John the Baptist. And her time
finally came!
    One day, Salome, the daughter of
Herodias, entertained Herod by dancing
for him on his birthday. Herod became so
excited with her dancing that he foolishly
promised to give Salome anything she
wanted.
    Salome decided to talk to her mother
before she made her request. She
probably had lots of ideas of what she
would like. But she wanted her mother to
help her decide what to ask for.
    "Ask for the head of John the Baptist
on a platter," the cruel woman told her
daughter.
    Salome returned to Herod with her
answer. It was not at all what he had
expected her to say. What should he do?
He could refuse her request. Breaking his
oath to her, he probably reasoned, would

not be as bad as murdering an innocent man who said he was sent from God.

But Herod was too weak to admit that he had made a mistake. He did not want to listen to what his wife would say if he refused this request. He did not know what the people around him would say if their ruler did not keep his word.

Herod ordered his men to carry out Salome's request.

When the disciples heard of the foul deed, they went to the prison to take the body of John the Baptist and bury it.

John the Baptist was dead. No longer would he preach the message of repentance.

But the message of God continued to be preached. God continued to change the lives of those who repented of their sins and turned to Jesus for salvation.

The Messiah had come! He told the way for man to be right with God.

People turned to Jesus because John the Baptist did his job. Because of John

the Baptist, people repented of their sins.
People were ready to listen to Jesus.
People were ready for Jesus to change
their lives.

"The voice crying in the wilderness"
had caused people throughout the land to
trust Jesus as Lord and Savior

Thinkback: Why did Herod kill John the
Baptist? List ways you know John finished
the work God called him to do.

Reflections

• John the Baptist came to prepare people for the coming of the Messiah. How do you think the people would have treated Jesus if John the Baptist had not come?

Who are some people you know that you could tell about Jesus? What are some ways you can be God's messenger?

• Not everyone liked what John the Baptist had to say. Some listened. Some believed. But Herod had him killed because of what he preached.

How can you know that what you are doing is right? Would you still do right if someone made fun of you for going to church, for reading your Bible, or for standing up for the right when no one else did?

• Herod liked John the Baptist. He had heard him preach. He believed John was a good man. But Herod had John killed because of a foolish promise. And Herod was too weak to admit he was wrong.

He refused to stand up for what he knew was right.

When you make a mistake, what do you do about it? What should you do?

● When Jesus came, John the Baptist lost most of his followers. Jesus became more popular with the people. John's work was finished. How do we know that John was not jealous of Jesus? Read John 1.

How do you act when someone else wins a game or gets more attention than you do? Who can help you get rid of jealous feelings?

● Most people have doubts once in a while. When John the Baptist had doubts, he took them to the right person. He took them to Jesus. John did not understand what was happening. But he looked to Jesus for the answer.

When you have doubts about God, about good and evil, about what is happening around you, where do you look for the answers to your questions? Jesus knows and understands you and can answer the questions you have.

• ROME

MACEDONIA PHILLIPPI •
THESSALONICA •
BEROEA

AEGEAN
SEA

TROAS

• ANTIOCH
LYSTRA • ICONIUM
• DERBE

ATHENS •

EPHESUS •

• ANTIOC

CYPRUS

SAMARIA

MEDITERRANEAN SEA

CAESAREA •
JOPPA •
AZOTUS •
GAZA •

JO
RIV

• JERUSAL

DEADSE

SOME NEW TESTAMENT PLACES

ETHIOPIA

48